CRIMINAL PROFILING

WRITTEN BY:
Rebecca Stefoff

Marshall Cavendish
Benchmark
New York

All websites were available and accurate when this book was sent to press.

LIBRARY OF CONGRESS CATALOGING-IN-PUBLICATION DATA
Stefoff, Rebecca
Criminal profiling / Rebecca Stefoff.
p. cm. — (Forensic science investigated ; 2)
Includes bibliographical references and index.
ISBN 978-0-7614-4141-0
1. Criminal behavior, Prediction of—Juvenile literature. 2. Criminal profilers—Juvenile literature. 3. Criminal investigation—Juvenile literature. I. Title.
HV8073.5.S755 2011
363.25'8—dc22
2010010535
EDITOR: Christina Gardeski   PUBLISHER: Michelle Bisson
ART DIRECTOR: Anahid Hamparian   SERIES DESIGNER: Kristen Branch

Photo Research by Lindsay Aveilhe
Cover photo by Newscom
The photographs in this book are used with permission and through the courtesy of: David W. Hamilton/Glow Images: p. 4; Robert Sherbow/Time Life Pictures/Getty Images: p. 7; Private Collection/© Look and Learn/The Bridgeman Art Library: p. 9; Private Collection/Peter Newark American Pictures/The Bridgeman Art Library International: p. 12; Mercury News: p. 16; Bettmann/Corbis: p. 18; Bibliotheque Nationale, Paris, France/Archives Charmet/The Bridgeman Art Library: pp. 21, 23; Popperfoto/Getty Images: p. 27; Apic/Getty Images: p. 29; Bettmann/Corbis: p. 31; Paul Sakuma/AP Photo: p. 35; Sami Sarkis/Getty Images: p. 38; Brian Atkinson/Alamy: p. 41; Hulton Archive/Getty Images: p. 43; Paul Rapson/Photo Researchers, Inc.: p. 47; Louise Murray/Photo Researchers, Inc.: p. 50; David Ellis-Pool/Getty Images: p. 52; Newscom: p. 55; Reuters/Corbis: p. 58; Kevin Irby/Getty Images: p. 61; Arthur Turner/Alamy: p. 63; Patti McConville: p. 67; Newscom: p. 68; Ann Cutting/Getty Images: p. 70; Newscom: p. 73; Ted Soqui/Corbis: p. 74; Kim Kulish/Corbis: p. 77; Liz Hafalia/San Francisco Chronicle/Corbis: p. 81.

Printed in Malaysia (T)
1 3 5 6 4 2
Cover: Profiling is one way of identifying the unknown offenders who commit crimes.

CONTENTS

The Trailside Killer attacked hikers in the rugged, majestic terrain of California's Point Reyes National Seashore Park.

WHAT IS
FORENSICS?

LAW ENFORCEMENT AGENCIES around San Francisco Bay were desperate for help as winter began in 1980. For more than a year a murderer had been striking down hikers in the area's parks. Newspapers called him the Trailside Killer. The list of victims kept growing, but the killer's identity remained a mystery.

Four murders had come to light on a single November day. Friends of Shauna May had reported the young woman missing when she failed to meet them as planned for a hike in Point Reyes National Seashore Park, north of San Francisco. Two days later searchers found May's body. Next to it lay the body of another young woman. Both had been murdered. But that wasn't all. Not far away the searchers found two more bodies, the remains of a nineteen-year-old man and his eighteen-year-old fiancée who had vanished while hiking six weeks earlier. The four bodies found that day brought the total of the Trailside Killer's victims to seven.

Police and sheriff's departments, as well as agents from the local offices of the Federal Bureau of Investigation (FBI) were working overtime, yet they had made little progress in identifying the killer. The local FBI office asked for help from FBI experts in Quantico, Virginia, not far from Washington, DC.

An FBI special agent named John Douglas answered the call and flew to California. At the sheriff's department in Marin County, across the Golden Gate Bridge from San Francisco, Douglas walked into a room filled with law enforcement officials who had been working on the Trailside Killer case for months. He was there to tell them what kind of criminal they were looking for.

The killer, Douglas told the crowd, was white and in his early thirties. He was intelligent, but he had spent time in prison, probably for sex crimes. He lived in the Bay Area and was shy, keeping to himself much of the time. He probably worked in a mechanical or industrial job. His background probably included fire starting or

▲ John Douglas examines crime scene evidence in this 1991 photograph of his office at the FBI training facility.

cruelty to animals. "Another thing," Douglas told his listeners, "the killer will have a speech impediment."

John Douglas was a criminal profiler, someone who studies a crime in order to describe the traits of the person responsible. At the time Douglas made his presentation about the Trailside Killer, **profiling** was new to many law enforcement officials, but the concept was rapidly gaining a place in the world of **forensic science**.

▶ FORENSICS AND CRIMINOLOGY

Forensic science is the use of scientific methods and tools to investigate crimes and bring suspects to trial. The term "forensic" comes from ancient Rome, where people debated matters of law in a public meeting place called the Forum. The Latin word *forum* gave rise to *forensic*, meaning "relating to courts of law or to public debate."

Today the term **forensics** has several meanings. One is the art of speaking in debates, which is why some schools have forensics clubs or teams for students who want to learn debating skills. The best-known meaning of "forensics," though, is crime solving through forensic science.

Fascination with forensics explains the popularity of many TV shows, movies, and books, but crime and

▲ Political enemies of Roman leader Julius Caesar plotted to end his rule—permanently. They stabbed him in a group attack.

science have been linked for a long time. The first science used in criminal investigation was medicine, and one of the earliest reports of forensic medicine comes from ancient Rome. In 44 BCE, the Roman leader Julius Caesar was stabbed to death not far from the Forum. A physician named Antistius examined the body and found that Caesar had received twenty-three stab wounds, but only one wound was fatal.

Antistius had performed one of history's first recorded postmortem examinations, in which a physician looks at a body to find out how the person died. But forensics has always had limits. Antistius could point out the chest wound that had killed Caesar, but he could not say who had struck the deadly blow.

Death in its many forms inspired the first forensic manuals. The oldest one was published in China in 1248. Called *Hsi duan yu* (The Washing Away of Wrongs), it tells how the bodies of people who have been strangled differ from drowning victims. When a corpse is recovered from the water, says the manual, officers of the law should examine the tissues and small bones in the neck. Torn tissues and broken bones show that the victim met with foul play before being thrown into the water.

Poison became another landmark in the history of forensics in 1813, when Mathieu Orfila, a professor of medical and forensic chemistry at the University of Paris, published *Traité des poisons* (A Treatise on Poisons). Orfila described the deadly effects of various mineral, vegetable, and animal substances. He laid the foundation of the modern science of **toxicology**, the branch of forensics that deals with poisons, drugs, and their effects on the human body.

As France's most famous expert on poisons, Orfila played a part in an 1840 criminal trial that received wide publicity. Marie LaFarge , a widow, was accused of having murdered her husband. Orfila testified that upon examining LaFarge's corpse, he had found arsenic in the stomach. Marie LaFarge insisted that she had not fed the arsenic to her husband, and therefore he must have eaten it while away from home. The court, however, sentenced her to life imprisonment. Pardoned in 1850 after ten years in prison, Marie LaFarge died the next year, claiming innocence to the end.

Cases such as the LaFarge trial highlighted the growing use of medical evidence in criminal investigations and trials. Courts were recognizing other kinds of forensic evidence, too. In 1784 a British murder case had been decided by physical evidence. The torn edge of a piece of newspaper found in the pocket of a suspect named John Toms matched the torn edge of a ball of paper found in the wound of a man who had been killed by a pistol shot to the head (at the time people used rolled pieces of cloth or paper, called wadding, to hold bullets firmly in gun barrels). Toms was declared guilty of murder. In 1835 an officer of Scotland Yard, Britain's famous police division, caught a murderer by using a flaw on the fatal bullet to trace the bullet to its maker. Such cases marked the birth of ballistics, the branch of forensics that deals with firearms and cartridges.

▲ The study of firearms and ammunition was helping to solve crimes by the time this Colt revolver was manufactured in the United States in 1860.

Not all forensic developments involved murder. Science also helped solve crimes such as arson and forgery. By the early nineteenth century, chemists had developed the first tests to identify certain dyes used in ink. Experts could then determine the age and chemical makeup of the ink on documents, such as wills and valuable manuscripts, that were suspected of being fakes.

Forensics started to become a regular part of police work at the end of the nineteenth century, after an

Austrian law professor named Hans Gross published a two-volume handbook on the subject in 1893. Gross's book, usually referred to as *Criminal Investigation*, brought together all the many techniques that scientists and law enforcers had developed for examining the physical evidence of crime—bloodstains, bullets, and more. Police departments started using *Criminal Investigation* to train officers. The book entered law school courses as well.

Modern forensics specialists regard Hans Gross as the founder of their profession. Among other contributions, Gross invented the word **criminalistics**. He used it to refer to the general study of crime or criminals. Today, however, criminalistics has a narrower, more specific meaning. It refers to the study of physical evidence from crime scenes. The study of crime, criminals, and criminal behavior is usually called **criminology**.

Profiling is one branch of criminology. It draws on **psychology**, which is the scientific study of the mind and of human behavior, and it also uses information provided by criminalists and forensic scientists who examine crime scenes and analyze **trace evidence**. A skilled profiler can tell a lot about a criminal from the evidence he or she leaves behind, as FBI profiler John Douglas showed when he described the killer who was haunting the Bay Area's hiking trails.

▶ THE TRAILSIDE KILLER

When Douglas said that the Trailside Killer would prove to have a speech impediment such as a stutter or stammer, one of the detectives in the room asked the FBI man how he could possibly know such a thing. Douglas's explanation was an example of profiling in action.

The Trailside Killer struck in secluded places, Douglas pointed out. He overpowered his victims quickly with force, rather than talking to them until they trusted him enough to accompany him. This made Douglas think that the killer had some kind of problem or disability that made him feel insecure and ashamed. Douglas ruled out a missing limb or other major physical handicap because the killer had clearly been able to control his victims, most of whom were fit and strong. And although eyewitnesses had described individuals who had been seen around some of the crime sites, none of the descriptions mentioned a noticeable physical feature such as a limp, a scar, or a birthmark. Douglas concluded that the Trailside Killer's weakness or handicap wasn't something you could see, yet it was something that would limit the killer's ability to be comfortable around other people— something like a speech impediment.

"I may be wrong about some things," Douglas said. "I may miss the age. I may miss the occupation or the IQ. But I'm certainly not going to miss the race or the sex, and . . . I'm not going to miss that he has some kind of defect that really bothers him. Maybe it's not a speech impediment, but I think it is."

In May 1981, a few months after Douglas presented his profile of the Trailside Killer, a young woman named Heather Scaggs disappeared. She had told friends that she was going to see a man who had a car for sale. The owner of the car, David Carpenter, taught people how to use industrial equipment such as printing machines. Scaggs was one of his students.

Police questioned Carpenter, then placed him in a lineup with other men who looked roughly like him. Several witnesses, including a survivor of one of the Trailside Killer's attacks, viewed the lineup and identified Carpenter as the murderer. He was arrested, tried, and eventually convicted of multiple **homicides**.

David Carpenter, the Trailside Killer, was fifty-one years old and white. He had a record of convictions for sex crimes before the murders began. He also had a severe stutter. According to one newspaper article about his trial, "Carpenter's face contorted and his head shook as he struggled to [answer a question]. He finally managed to utter a 'yes' after the passage of several seconds." As a child, Carpenter had been taunted by other children because of his speech impediment, and he had been cruel to animals. Nearly all the points in Douglas's profile had turned out to be correct.

▲ David Carpenter, the Trailside Killer, stuttered—as the profiler had predicted. In 2010, DNA evidence tied him to another victim: a Montana woman killed in California in 1979.

Not all profiles are as detailed, or as accurate, as Douglas's profile of the Trailside Killer. Even the most detailed and accurate profile does not help solve a case if investigators cannot come up with suspects. As a resource for law enforcement, however, profiling can narrow the pool of possible suspects, helping police or FBI agents to better focus their attention and resources. A profiler may also give police and **prosecutors** tips on how to interview or question suspects. And sometimes, at its best, profiling produces clues that lead straight to a criminal.

Cesare Lombroso, an Italian doctor, thought that a criminal's true nature revealed itself in physical features.

CHAPTER ONE

THE ORIGINS OF
PROFILING

▼ CRIMINAL PROFILERS HAVE BECOME

heroic, glamorous figures. Movies, TV shows, and books have glorified the role of profilers in tracking down serial killers, child abusers, and kidnappers. Yet these productions do not always paint an accurate picture of how criminal profiling works, and often they neglect to mention its shortcomings. Typically, they do not even explain clearly what profiling means.

Profiling is an approach to solving a crime by asking, "What does this crime say about the person who committed it?" The scientific study of crime and criminals began in the nineteenth century, when some early criminologists tried to pinpoint the features of the typical offender. Today criminologists continue to study crime and criminals, with three main goals. One goal is to understand why people commit crimes. Another is to classify criminal behavior, which means analyzing it and sorting it into categories. The third goal is to solve crimes, and that is the purpose of profiling.

▶ THE MARK OF THE CRIMINAL

Early criminologists thought that while some people became criminals as a result of accident or circumstances, others were "fated to be criminals." The idea was that these unfortunate individuals had a greater than average chance of committing crimes because they had mental or physical weaknesses, limitations, or flaws. Certain criminologists also believed that people who became criminals possessed visible traits or qualities. If those qualities could be identified, experts could use them to recognize potential criminals. It might be possible to predict criminal behavior, or even to prevent it.

One of the first researchers to delve into the roots of criminal behavior was an Italian doctor named Cesare Lombroso. After measuring the skulls of 383 dead Italian convicts and gathering information about their crimes, Lombroso sorted the skulls by type of crime and by the convict's age, sex, level of education, and physical features. Lombroso also considered

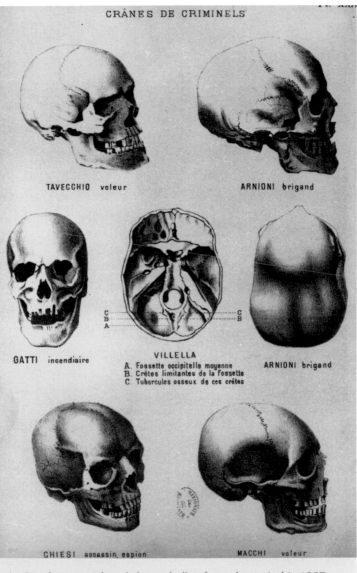

CRÂNES DE CRIMINELS

TAVECCHIO voleur

ARNIONI brigand

GATTI incendiaire

VILLELLA
A. Fossette occipitelle moyenne
B. Crêtes limitantes de la fossette
C. Tubercules osseux de ces crêtes

ARNIONI brigand

CHIESI assassin, espion

MACCHI voleur

▲ Lombroso analyzed these skulls of murderers in his 1887 book *L'Homme Criminel* (The Criminal Man).

geographic location and other characteristics of the crime and its perpetrator. From this data he developed theories that he published in 1876, in a book titled *The Criminal Man.*

According to Lombroso, there were three main kinds of criminals: insane, criminaloid, and born. In his system, insane criminals were mentally or physically ill or deformed. Criminaloids did not have recognizable defects, but Lombroso believed that they were mentally and emotionally unstable and could become criminals under the right (or wrong) circumstances. Born criminals, in his view, were primitive individuals who were less highly evolved than ordinary people. Lombroso listed eighteen physical features that he had observed on individuals he considered to be born criminals. The signs included a large jaw or large cheekbones, ears bigger or smaller than normal, a large number of wrinkles on the face, abnormal teeth, and long arms. Someone with five or more of these sinister traits, said Lombroso, could be said to be a born criminal.

Other criminologists shared Lombroso's basic idea that at least some criminals could be recognized by their physical appearance. Certain physical traits, in other words, were believed to be signs of a criminal nature. In 1914 an American writer named Gerald Fosbroke claimed in a book, *Character Reading through Analysis of the Features*, that a person's nature is revealed in his

Fig. 7. Tipo comune (a lunga faccia) - Uxoricida.

Fig. 10. Tipo comune (a grande mascella) - Omicida.

Fig. 8. Tipo comune (a lunga faccia) - Omicida-ladro.

Fig. II. Tipo comune (a grande mascella) - Assassino.

Fig. 9. Tipo comune (a grande mascella) - Omicida-ladro.

Fig. 12 Tipo comune (a grande mascella) - Assassino.

▲ With faulty logic, Lombroso claimed that the facial characteristics he had observed in some criminals were signs of what he termed "born criminals."

or her face. He wrote, "As our characters form, our faces evolve, upon them is written largely the story of what we are, whether strong or weak, for those who will to read." According to this view, an observer can tell just from looking at someone's features what kind of character traits, including criminal traits, the person possesses. "Character analysis," as Fosbroke's ideas were called, has no scientific basis and has fallen out of fashion today.

In the 1950s German criminologist Ernst Kretschmer published criminological theories that, he claimed, were based on a study of more than 4,400 criminals. He classified criminals into four groups according to body type. Tall, thin criminals usually were said to be involved in theft and fraud, for example, while athletic ones were linked to violent crimes. Kretschmer did not make his research data public, and he did not compare criminals with noncriminals. For those reasons, his ideas could not be regarded as scientifically proven, and few people took them seriously.

Criminological theories like those of Lombroso and Kretschmer suggested that the right key or code would instantly unlock the mysteries of the criminal character, letting society identify and control its most dangerous members. Such theories themselves are dangerous, however. It has never been proven that criminals share certain recognizable traits, but even if they did, it would not be right to think that everyone with those traits was a criminal, or would become one.

Attempts to show a connection between physical features and criminal behavior ran the risk of creating prejudice against people who happened to look a particular way but were completely innocent. Fortunately, criminologists developed other ways of studying the origins of crime and the relationships between criminals and their deeds.

▶ WHAT DOES THE EVIDENCE SAY?

Around the time criminologists such as Lombroso launched the study of criminal behavior, police and detectives began making more careful, systematic examinations of crime scenes and evidence. In the late nineteenth century, after Hans Gross published *Criminal Investigation*, law enforcement groups around the world devoted new energy to collecting and interpreting evidence. Modern forensic science was under way, and investigators began to use new tools. One of those tools was profiling.

A series of five gruesome murders in London in 1888 led to one of the first well-known examples of profiling, although that term would not be used until nearly a century later. The 1888 case has become one of the most famous mysteries in criminal history. The

SHERLOCK HOLMES IS THE MOST famous detective who *never* existed. Holmes was the fictional creation of British writer Sir Arthur Conan Doyle, who published his first tale about the great detective in 1887. Among other things, Holmes was what we would now call a profiler. In many of Conan Doyle's stories, the detective examines a crime scene or an object and then, to the amazement of his sidekick, Dr. John Watson, reels off a detailed description of the unknown criminal, or the object's owner.

Inventing a crime-solving genius wasn't Conan Doyle's only brush with criminology. The author also investigated several real-life criminal cases in the early twentieth century. One involved George Edalji, an English lawyer whose father was from India. Someone was mutilating and killing livestock near the attorney's country town. Anonymous letters accused Edalji, and in 1903 he was tried, found guilty, and sentenced to prison for the crimes.

Many people protested that the case against Edalji was weak. They felt that he had been falsely accused and convicted because of racial prejudice. Conan Doyle heard about the case and read all the police reports. It was clear to him that Edalji could not be guilty. Forensic evidence, such as soil samples from Edalji's boots, failed to link him to the crimes—which continued after he was arrested! Conan Doyle wrote a series of articles about the case for the *Daily Telegraph*, a newspaper that was widely read throughout the United Kingdom. After the famous author

pointed out the striking flaws in the prosecution's case, Edalji was cleared of the crimes, released from prison, and allowed to practice law again.

Conan Doyle later tackled another miscarriage of justice. A German immigrant named Oscar Slater had been convicted and imprisoned for murdering an old woman in Edinburgh, Scotland. Conan Doyle took an interest in the matter and discovered that the police and prosecutors had done a shockingly poor job of investigating the case. Among other lapses, the police had failed to investigate Slater's alibi. Although Slater said that he was home with his girlfriend at the time of the killing, prosecutors had ignored this claim—which later turned out to be true, supported by an independent witness.

Much evidence pointed to Slater's innocence. Nearly twenty years after his imprisonment, thanks to publicity drummed up by Conan Doyle, Slater was set free and his conviction was overturned.

In Sherlock Holmes, Conan Doyle created a detective gifted with sharp-eyed observation and clear, logical thinking. When Conan Doyle applied those same qualities to real cases, he demonstrated a key principle of forensic science: Let the evidence speak.

five victims were prostitutes, and their killer—whose identity remains unknown to this day—called himself Jack the Ripper.

Doctors who worked for the police studied the victims' bodies, looking for clues that would help police catch the killer. In the end, the doctors disagreed about a key point: whether or not the killer was skilled in cutting up bodies.

Dr. Thomas Bond, a physician who held the post of police surgeon and helped the London police on many cases, felt that the mutilations of the women's bodies showed no sign of skill or expert knowledge. The killer, in other words, was not a surgeon or a butcher of animals. But another police surgeon, Dr. George Phillips, thought differently after examining the body of Annie Chapman. Like the bodies of several other victims, Chapman's corpse was missing some internal organs. The physicians agreed that the organs had been removed after the murder, not before. Phillips, however, believed that Chapman's organs had been taken out by a skilled or experienced person, meaning that the killer was likely to be a doctor, surgeon, or butcher. (Another possibility is that the killer had learned how to take bodies apart by experimenting on earlier, unknown victims.)

Despite their differences of opinion, the various doctors who examined Jack the Ripper's victims shared the same basic approach to the task: to build a profile of

▲ The world was fascinated by Jack the Ripper, who murdered women in the streets of London. A 1909 French magazine used an image of Sherlock Holmes (upper left) to sell a story about the Ripper.

the killer based on the evidence of his crimes. As one **medical examiner** said at the time, the state of the bodies "may suggest the character of the man who did it."

▶ AN EARLY PROFILE: THE MAD BOMBER

A modern case that featured profiling took place in New York City in the mid-twentieth century. The case began to unfold in the early 1940s, when two small bombs were found near the headquarters of Consolidated Edison (Con Ed), the company that supplied the city with electricity. Notes to the police and Con Ed threatened to make the company pay for some unnamed wrong it had committed, but no details were given. The United States then became involved in World War II, and the notes and bombs stopped—for a while.

In 1950 bombs began turning up in phone booths around the city, in theaters, train stations, and other public places. These bombs were larger than the first two, and many of them exploded. Panic gripped New York. The police were unable to get a lead on the so-called Mad Bomber. In 1956 they sought advice from Dr. James Brussel.

Brussel's medical specialty was **psychiatry**, the treatment of mental and emotional disorders. He examined copies of the Mad Bomber's letters, noticing the neat lettering and the slightly stiff, old-fashioned wording. Then he told the police officers what kind of

▲ New York police arrest George Metesky, who was later
convicted as the Mad Bomber. A psychologist had predicted
Metesky's double-breasted suit.

person they should be looking for. According to Brussel's published version of the case, he said that the Mad Bomber was mature and orderly, with some education. He was unmarried and probably lived with a sister, aunt, or other woman who was like a mother to him. He was a Slav, a person of Eastern European descent. Brussel believed that the letter writer would favor proper, conservative clothing, so he predicted that when the bomber was caught he would be wearing a double-breasted suit with the jacket buttoned.

Meanwhile, a search through Con Ed's old personnel files revealed a letter that had been written more than twenty years earlier by George Metesky, a former employee with a grudge against the company. Metesky's signed letter contained phrases that had appeared in the Mad Bomber's taunting letters. The police located Metesky and, in 1957, arrested him for the bombings. Metesky, who was later convicted of the Mad Bomber's crimes, was a mature, tidy, unemployed, unmarried man of Slavic descent who lived with his sisters. When officers showed up at the house to arrest Metesky, he put on a double-breasted suit and buttoned the jacket.

▶ THE FBI'S PROFILERS

Profiling became established as a formal tool of crime investigation in the 1970s, largely due to the work of Howard Teten at the Federal Bureau of Investigation.

After nearly a decade as a California police officer, Teten joined the FBI. As an FBI special agent he studied forensic science and also researched the psychological aspects of crime and criminals with Dr. Brussel, the psychiatrist who had profiled the Mad Bomber.

In 1970, Teten began teaching an FBI course in applied criminology. A key part of the course was building a picture of an unidentified offender, a process that soon became known as profiling. Over the next several years, Teten and another FBI instructor named Pat Mullany included profiling techniques in the criminology courses they taught.

THE BEHAVIORAL SCIENCE UNIT

In 1972, the FBI opened a new department called the Behavioral Science Unit, or BSU, at the Quantico office. The behavioral sciences are the sciences that study how people behave, as individuals (psychology) and in groups or societies (sociology). The purpose of the BSU was to apply ideas and knowledge from the behavioral sciences to the investigation of major crimes.

Serial crimes were the focus of the BSU. Serial crimes are strings of similar offenses—rapes or murders, for example—committed by one person, sometimes all in one city, sometimes spread out across multiple states. Serial crimes can be especially hard to solve because the offenders usually attack strangers. As a result, police cannot find leads among the victims' families and acquaintances.

Teten and Mullany were part of the original BSU. Other early members of the unit included Roy Hazelwood, Robert Ressler, and John Douglas, all of whom have written books about their experiences as profilers. Members of the unit performed research, taught criminology, and assisted with cases that were being investigated by various FBI offices and police departments. As departments that had benefited from the BSU's services spread the word, the unit's reputation grew. Team members frequently traveled around the country to view crime scenes, to meet with local law enforcement personnel, and to create profiles.

Since the early years of the BSU, the division of the FBI that focuses on criminal profiling has been reorganized several times. Today the agents who serve as profilers are part of the FBI's National Center for the Analysis of Violent Crime, or NCAVC, based at Quantico. They provide training and assistance for federal, state, and local law enforcement agencies.

TRACKING CRIME AND CRIMINALS

NCAVC is made up of several units. One is the Violent Criminal Apprehension Program, called ViCAP. This division of the FBI collects information about violent crimes from law enforcement agencies at all levels

▲ A police officer reviews predators' methods of storing information. Computers and databases play key roles in police
work and in profiling.

around the country. The information becomes part of a
vast computer database that lets agents sort crimes by
date, methods, crime scene details, and other features.

Using the ViCAP database, law enforcement officials in different **jurisdictions** can connect crimes that
are widely separated in space and time. For example, if
the knot used to tie a homicide victim in Texas is an
exact match to the knots used three years ago in similar crimes in Illinois, and nine years ago in Missouri,
the same killer may have been operating in all three
states. Pooling data on all the cases may give the investigators of each homicide new information—and
possibly help them identify and capture the killer.

The Child Abduction and Serial Murder Investigative Resources Center (CASMIRC) is another part of NCAVC. This unit focuses on crimes against children, including murder, kidnapping, and mysterious disappearances. CASMIRC maintains a database similar to ViCAP, but its work is limited to child-related crimes. This unit of the FBI also provides training and help with active investigations.

PROFILING OFFENDERS

The third arm of NCAVC is the Behavioral Analysis Unit (BAU). The members of this unit provide a variety of services to investigators at the local, state, and federal levels. One of these services is developing profiles of unknown offenders. The BAU is home to the FBI's working profilers, although the FBI does not use the term "profiler." Within the FBI, the process of reviewing the facts of a crime and interpreting the criminal's characteristics is called criminal investigative analysis. The men and women who develop offender profiles are called supervisory special agents.

The Behavioral Science Unit (BSU) now belongs to an FBI training department. The staff of this department teaches elements of the behavioral sciences to FBI agents, military and intelligence officers, and law enforcement officers. The BSU describes its subject this way: "Behavioral science is all about better understanding criminals and terrorists—who they are, how they think, why they do what they do—as a means to help solve crimes and prevent attacks." As taught by the BSU, behavioral science includes criminal investigative analysis, or profiling.

Profiling today is not limited to the FBI. Other law enforcement agencies in the United States and around the world have departments that perform behavioral analysis, or offender profiling. Individuals, organizations, and investigative companies also offer profiling services. Their clients include not only police and sheriff's departments but also businesses and private clients. Many of the people who work as profilers outside formal law enforcement are former FBI agents or police officers. Some are criminologists or psychologists with backgrounds in research rather than in law enforcement.

Profiling is always aimed at the same goal: to discover things about an unknown person by studying his or her behavior. Profilers, however, approach this challenge in different ways.

Casting light on the shadowy figure of an unknown offender is the challenge faced by criminal profilers.

CHAPTER TWO

PROFILERS
AT WORK

▼ PROFILING IS STILL BEING DEFINED.

Profilers have different ideas about how to create profiles, and even about what their practice should be called. Some profilers regard what they do as an art or a skill, born of experience and instinct. Occasionally they use language that makes profiling sound mysterious—"seeing into the criminal's mind" or "looking through the criminal's eyes." Other profilers are striving to establish their discipline as a scientific profession, with clear-cut standards, guidelines, and training. At the same time, criminologists and law enforcement officers sometimes disagree about the value of profiles. A few critics have questioned whether profiling has genuine meaning or usefulness.

By any name or definition, profiling begins with a crime, then proceeds to describe the unknown person or persons who committed the offense. Using information about similar crimes, or drawing entirely on the evidence from the specific crime scene, a profiler develops a picture of the offender, who is sometimes called the **unsub** (for "unknown subject"). The purpose of the picture is to help law enforcement identify the offender and bring him or her to justice.

▶ APPROACHES TO PROFILING

There are various approaches to criminal profiling. One approach is to compare the crime to what is already known about similar crimes and the people who committed them. A profiler who chooses this approach might use statistics about criminal behavior to interpret the unsub's characteristics.

Statistics are simply pieces of information that have been gathered, sorted, and organized. In a case of arson, or deliberate fire setting, for example, a profiler could refer to a report from the federal Department of Justice that says that 52 percent—more than half—of the people arrested for setting fires in a given year were under the age of eighteen. Based on this information, the profiler might look at a new, unsolved arson case and say, "There's a good chance our unsub is a kid or teenager."

▲ Fire devours a farmhouse. Profilers know that arson, the deliberate setting of fires, is a crime often committed by young people.

THE CRIMINAL PROFILING PROJECT

The statistical approach to profiling got its start in the late 1970s. John Douglas and Robert Ressler, two of the FBI's early profilers, were teaching a short course in applied criminology at police departments across the country. In class they discussed well-known criminals, such as Charles Manson, who directed his followers to commit murders in Los Angeles, and Edmund Kemper, who had killed his mother, other family members, and several female hitchhikers.

Manson and Kemper were alive and in prison, as were other criminals whose cases the agents reviewed in their course. Douglas and Ressler wondered whether interviewing the killers would give insights into their behavior—insights that could help identify offenders who committed similar crimes. Douglas recalls saying to his partner, "Let's see if we can talk to them; ask them why they did it, what it was like through *their* eyes."

That was the start of the FBI's Criminal Profiling Project. Between 1979 and 1983 agents interviewed 36 offenders who had a total of 118 known victims. Some of the criminals were serial killers whose crimes stretched over time. Others were spree killers, who had murdered multiple victims in a single bloody out-burst. Still others had committed double or single homicide. All were adult males, and so they did not represent a complete sample of all violent criminals.

▲ Profiling moved forward in the 1970s when criminologists studied convicted killers such as Charles Manson. Manson's 1969 mug shot was taken by the Los Angeles police.

From data gathered during the Criminal Profiling Project, FBI analysts developed early tools for classifying offenders by the features of crimes and crime scenes. Since that time the FBI has interviewed many other convicted criminals, including hijackers and persons involved in armed robbery. In addition, the bureau has collected data on thousands of crimes through ViCAP and other centralized reporting systems.

ORGANIZED OR DISORGANIZED?

One of the first tools to come out of the Criminal Profiling Program was the "organized/disorganized" checklist. A crime was categorized as organized or disorganized based on the evidence. Signs of careful planning, for example, indicated an organized crime. So did the hiding of a victim's body. A disorganized crime, in contrast, appeared to be spontaneous or unplanned, and the body was not hidden.

Just as crimes were either organized or disorganized, so were criminals. Based on information gathered about convicted criminals, the FBI developed a list of the traits of each type of offender. An organized criminal was likely to be of average or above-average intelligence, tended to have a sense of superiority to other people, and often lived with a spouse or partner. This type of killer rarely left behind a weapon or a revealing clue. A disorganized criminal, in contrast, would probably have below-average intelligence, would feel inferior, and would live alone or with parents. Such a criminal might make mistakes such as leaving behind a murder weapon or other clue.

Criminologists and psychologists soon pointed out limitations in the organized/disorganized system of classifying crimes and offenders. Not all crime scenes, or all offenders, fit neatly into one category. The classifications were based on a very small sample of criminals, and the data had not been collected in a controlled, scientific way. In recent years the FBI and other profilers have begun to move away from the simple "organized or disorganized" classification. Investigators now recognize that many crimes and criminals fall somewhere between these two extremes.

BEHAVIORAL EVIDENCE ANALYSIS

Facts and statistics about known criminals are one source of information for a profiler. Another starting point is the evidence, which includes the crime scene, the victim, and any clues or traces left behind by the criminal. Some criminologists think that profiling should rest only on the details of each individual case, rather than on statistics and the general characteristics of groups, because there will always be individual offenders who do not match the group.

Profiling should be based strictly on the evidence, according to Brent Turvey, a forensic psychologist who helped found the Academy of Behavioral Profiling in 1999. Turvey favors an approach called behavioral evidence analysis (BEA), which focuses on the details of the crime. Instead of making predictions about the criminal based on statistics, averages, or statements about the "typical" offender, a profiler using BEA is limited to making deductions that are based on specific pieces of evidence.

▶ PUTTING TOGETHER A PROFILE

Profilers carry out their task in different ways, but all of them pay attention to certain important elements of each case. The following subjects and questions are usually part of the profiling process.

FORENSIC EVIDENCE

What has been revealed by the scientific analysis of the evidence? Footprints, blood spatter patterns, and trace evidence such as hair and carpet fiber left on a victim's body or at a crime scene may tell investigators a lot about the offender. Footprints, for example, contain details about the shoes a person wore and suggest the person's probable size. In addition, the depth, angle, and spacing of the prints can indicate whether the offender was standing, pacing, carrying something, or running. These clues to behavior may give a profiler insights into the criminal's state of mind.

Most profilers are not specialists in collecting and analyzing forensic evidence. Ideally, those tasks are performed by criminalists who are trained in the scientific handling and examination of materials. Once the forensic specialists have analyzed the evidence, the profiler receives the results. Depending upon the case, a profiler may receive many forensic reports covering

▲ A shoe print at a crime scene will be processed—collected and analyzed—by a criminalist. Later, a profiler may draw on the criminalist's report to paint a picture of the offender.

such topics as ballistics, toxicology (the analysis of drugs, poisons, or medications found in the victim or at the scene), and trace evidence analysis.

AUTOPSY

The state of a body—or a victim who survived an attack—is a source of important information about the offender. When someone dies as the result of a criminal attack, a medical examiner performs an **autopsy** on the remains. In many cases, an autopsy establishes the time and cause of death. It may help the profiler answer these questions: What type of weapon did the attacker use? Were the victim's injuries caused by someone wielding a weapon with skill and experience, or did the murderer shoot or stab at random? Was the victim tortured before death? Mutilated after death? Gruesome as they are, such questions may shed light on the offender's motives and fantasies.

VICTIMOLOGY

Details about the victim, whether alive or dead, can lead to information about the offender. The study of these details, a form of profiling in its own right, is called **victimology**. Profilers consider such questions as these: Had the victim received threats or spoken of having trouble with anyone? Did the victim follow a set routine that could have been observed by strangers? In cases of serial crimes, do the victims fall into a pattern, perhaps sharing characteristics such as age or hair color?

CRIME SCENE RECONSTRUCTION

Profiling requires an understanding of the events that took place and the order in which they occurred. To reconstruct a crime, a criminologist or profiler pulls together all available evidence. This includes not just forensic reports but also any documentary evidence, such as notes left by the offender or video from surveillance cameras. Another source of information is statements from a surviving victim, from any witnesses, and from people in the area or neighborhood who saw or heard something possibly related to the crime.

This material allows the crime to be pictured just as it unfolded. A profiler uses reconstruction to try to answer certain questions: Did the offender catch the victim by surprise or lure the victim into a dangerous situation? What risks did the offender take when committing the crime—in other words, how great were the chances that the offender would be seen, prevented from completing the crime, or caught in the act?

The profiler also wants to know if the attack happened quickly or slowly, and if the victim was killed in the same place the body was found. If the offender moved the body to a "dump site" after death, would a vehicle have been necessary? Overall, does the crime show evidence of planning, or signs that the offender was nervous, panicky, or remorseful? Finally, the profiler determines whether the offender needed special knowledge or skills, such as awareness that a particular building happened to be unoccupied, or how to disconnect an alarm system.

▲ Investigators can now use computer imaging software to reconstruct a three-dimensional graphic of a crime scene.

MODUS OPERANDI

The Latin phrase *modus operandi* means "method of operating." In crime investigation it is often short-ened to MO, and it refers to the way in which a crime was committed. An offender's MO is a set of behaviors that help the offender complete the crime, get away from the scene, and avoid detection. The MO might include such elements as working with an accomplice or partner, restraining a victim with handcuffs or rope, stealing a getaway car, or wearing a mask and gloves. A picture of the MO emerges from the forensic evidence, the autopsy report, the victimology review, and crime scene reconstruction.

The MO may be a link among different crimes committed by the same offender. However, an MO may change over time as the offender gains confi-dence and experience, picks up tips from the media or other criminals (this often happens during prison terms), experiences mental illness, or is affected by substance abuse.

THE PROFILE

Reports prepared by profilers differ in the level of detail provided. The most thorough profiles are deliv-ered in written form and contain not just the profiler's predictions or conclusions but also the evidence on which those conclusions are based.

▲ Documentary evidence, such as this taunting letter left by a sniper at the scene of a 2003 shooting, can provide valuable clues to profilers.

Most profiles include statements about the offender's likely gender, race, and age (either chronological or emotional). Many also include conclusions about the offender's education, line of work, and marital status (that is, whether the offender is single, married, divorced, or widowed).

Profilers also may consider whether the offender is a "loner" or interacts well with people, whether the offender is mentally ill (or perhaps experiencing a worsening of an existing mental state), whether the offender has committed earlier crimes, and whether the offender is likely to follow media reports of the case or try to become part of the investigation (for example, by hanging around crime scenes or coming forward as a witness).

BEYOND INVESTIGATION

Describing an unknown offender in an unsolved case is only part of what a profiler may be asked to do. After the investigation is over and authorities have identified a suspect, the profiler can analyze the suspect, then share with the police any insights about the suspect's behavior and psychology. These insights may help police strike the right tone in an interview, or ask questions that are likely to get the suspect talking. A profiler may suggest, for example, that a suspect might be inclined to open up to an interrogator who acts friendly, or that questions about the suspect's childhood might break down the suspect's defenses.

Once a person has been charged with the crime, the profiler may provide similar help to the prosecutor's office. Profilers or forensic psychologists may also be asked to testify at parole hearings about a convicted offender's behavior, mental state, and likelihood of committing further crimes if released.

WHAT DOES IT TAKE to become an FBI profiler? Although "profiler" is not an official FBI job title, criminal profiling is one duty of the supervisory special agents who are assigned to the Bureau's Behavioral Analysis Unit (BAU). The BAU, in turn, is part of the National Center for the Analysis of Violent Crime (NCAVC)—and getting a job in NCAVC is not easy.

To be hired by the NCAVC, a man or woman must first serve as an FBI special agent in another division of the bureau. To become FBI special agents, candidates must meet a set of requirements. They must be at least twenty-three years old, with a four-year college or university degree, a valid driver's license, and a minimum of three years' general work experience. They must pass a background investigation that includes a polygraph test (sometimes wrongly called a "lie-detector" test), as well as interviews with family members, teachers, neighbors, and employers. Candidates must also meet certain standards of physical fitness.

Becoming a special agent is not easy. Getting a job in the NCAVC is harder still. To work in the NCAVC, a special agent must have at least three years of experience in some other part of the FBI. But because there is a great deal of competition for NCAVC jobs, most people who are accepted into that unit have eight years or more of experience as special agents. During those years they gained experience investigating violent crimes, especially murder, rape, child kidnapping, and threats. Once accepted into the NCAVC, they take a 16-week training course that covers general

topics, such as criminal psychology and forensic science, but also includes more detailed instruction in areas like recovering bodies, evaluating threats, and conducting interviews with suspects.

Experience as an investigator is the most important qualification for anyone who wants to work as a special agent in the NCAVC, but it also helps to have an advanced degree in behavioral or forensic science. And for other staff positions in the NCAVC, such as a crime analyst or a research specialist, an advanced degree and professional training are essential.

Working in the NCAVC is not a 9-to-5 desk job. On any given day, a special agent or staff member might spend ten quiet hours in the office, reviewing crime scene photos, writing reports, and meeting with investigators to discuss cases. At any moment, though, an emergency call about a new case, a bomb threat, or a hostage situation may summon special agents and staff to a phone conference or a crime scene. And when the workday is finally done, a criminal profiler might find it impossible to relax, put the job out of mind, and enjoy the good things in life. Law enforcement is necessary and honorable work, but a job focused on violence, cruelty, and tragedy is not for everyone.

▶ DOES PROFILING WORK?

Movies and TV shows have made criminal profiling look exciting—and successful. The results achieved by profilers in these stories sometimes seem almost miraculous. In real life, however, some observers who have studied the profession wonder how well profiling really works.

Remember the case of the Mad Bomber of New York? Psychiatrist James Brussel told police what he had concluded about the person committing the crimes, and when George Metesky was finally caught, he matched the description Brussel had given, right down to the double-breasted suit.

For decades forensics experts have called the Metesky case a triumph of profiling and a milestone in criminology. But in a 2000 book called *Author Unknown*, literary researcher Don Foster questioned the accuracy of Brussel's Mad Bomber profile. According to Foster, Brussel actually told the police that the bomber would be German, would have a facial scar, and would hold a night job. None of these predictions fit Metesky.

Did Brussel change details of his profile to make it appear more accurate when he published his version of the story after Metesky's arrest? Whether or not Brussel tinkered with the truth, his Mad Bomber profile raises a larger question. Is profiling a genuine contribution to criminology, or is it simply a guessing game?

Psychological researcher Malcolm Gladwell thinks that profiling amounts to little more than a clever stunt, not too different from the "mind-reading" acts of performers. In a 2007 article about profiling, Gladwell claimed that "Brussel did not really understand the mind of the Mad Bomber. He seems to have understood only that, if you make a great number of predictions, the ones that were wrong will soon be forgotten, and the ones that turn out to be true will make you famous."

Profiles in some major cases have turned out to be spectacularly wrong. The Green River case was a series of forty-nine killings in the Pacific Northwest, beginning in 1982. A profile developed that year by John Douglas of the FBI did not lead to an arrest. The case remained unsolved for many years.

When investigators reopened the Green River case in 2001, they solved it by using DNA evidence that had been collected years earlier from a suspect named Gary L. Ridgway. Investigators also learned that Ridgway had written a taunting letter to a newspaper back in 1984. The letter wasn't signed, and instead of printing it, the newspaper turned it over to police. The letter might well have contained clues that would have

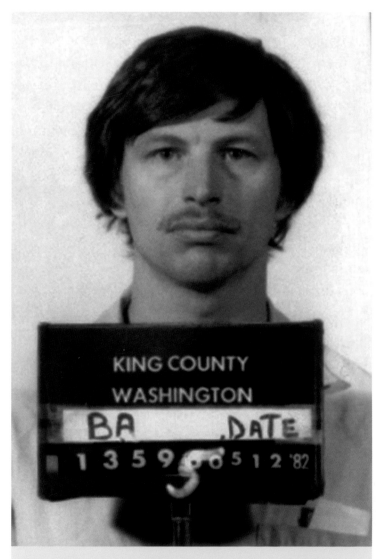

▲ In 1982, police in Washington state took this photo of Gary Ridgway, a suspect in the Green River murders. Nearly twenty years later Ridgway was identified as the killer.

led police to Ridgway—however, profiler Douglas declared the anonymous communication to be a false confession, sent by someone "who has no connection with the Green River homicides."

Failures such as the Green River case raise the question, "Does profiling work?" In reality, two questions are asked. First, is profiling accurate? Second, if it *is* accurate, does it help catch criminals and solve cases? A few researchers have begun studying the accuracy of profiling, as well as its usefulness. So far the results are uneven.

ACCURACY

The accuracy of profiles is hard to measure. One forensic psychologist who has examined the question is Laurence Alison of the University of Liverpool in Britain. Alison has found that many profiles contain statements so vague or general that they could apply to almost anyone, such as "The offender has had difficult relationships with the opposite sex." Other statements, such as "The offender fantasized about the crime for weeks before committing it," cannot be tested or proved and are basically meaningless.

What about more specific points of description, such as age? Alison and other researchers conducted experiments to test how people rate profiles. In one test they gave two groups of police officers the details of a real murder case. The officers also received a profile that Alison and his colleagues had written based on the details of the case. The profile covered six major features of the offender, including age and relationship to the victim.

The officers were then asked to compare that profile with a description of the offender, who had been caught. But only half the officers received a description of the real offender. The other half received a made-up description that differed from the real information in a number of ways—including the six major features that had been covered in the profile. In each group of police officers, more than half officers rated the profile as an accurate match with the description. The officers who got the made-up description of the offender were as likely to approve of the profile as those who got the real description, even though the two descriptions were completely different. This result may mean that the officers tended to see vague or even inaccurate statements as "fitting" the facts when those statements were made in the form of a criminal profile.

In another experiment, Alison and his colleagues used an FBI murder case and the actual profile that had been developed by the FBI during the investigation. Once again they provided two different offender descriptions. One described the real criminal, the

▲ Mug shots and fingerprints are keys to identifying specific individuals. To find individual suspects, however, law enforcement may use profiles to narrow the field of possibilities.

other was fake. Half the subjects in this study were police officers, and half were forensic professionals, people who worked in the criminal justice system or as criminal psychologists or psychiatrists. Half the people in each group received the real offender description. The other half received the fake one.

More than 50 percent of both the police officers and the forensic professionals rated the profile as generally or very accurate, regardless of whether they compared it with the real offender or the fake one. Another 25 percent rated it as somewhat accurate, again regardless of whether they saw the real offender or the fake.

Alison concluded that the subjects of the experiment tended to focus on the "hits" that seemed correct and to downplay the incorrect "misses." When rating the profile's accuracy, they gave the hits more weight than the misses. In addition, the police and forensic professionals who took part in Alison's experiment might have tended to view "official" profiles as accurate or authoritative, no matter what information they contained.

In an Australian experiment police officers were given a profile to review. Some officers were told that the document was the work of professional profilers. Others were told that the profile was written by "someone the investigator consulted." The same profile was used in all cases, but officers who believed that it had been written by a professional profiler rated it as more accurate than the other officers did. This suggests that how police evaluate a profile is related to the source of the document, not to what it says.

USEFULNESS

Even if a profile is accurate, is it useful? Does it help the police catch the criminal? That question has been studied in connection with a well-known early triumph of the FBI profilers. In 1979 a young woman named Francine Elveson was beaten and strangled to death in the stairway of the New York

▲ Profilers should focus only on details from the crime scene, says an approach to profiling that is called behavioral evidence analysis.

City apartment building where she lived with her parents. Afterward the killer carried Elveson's body to the roof, mutilated it, and staged the crime scene—that is, deliberately arranged the body and placed objects on and around it.

Local police interviewed more than two thousand potential witnesses and suspects but made little progress. They went to Quantico to seek help from the FBI profilers, carrying with them all of the crime scene reports and photos. The result was an offender profile that included these points:

- The killer lived close by (he knew his way around the building)
- The victim probably knew the killer, at least by sight (she did not scream or struggle)
- The killer was unemployed or had a low-paying night job (he was able to hang around and commit a murder while other people, including Elveson, were going to work)
- The killer probably lived with his parents or other relatives (he would be unable to afford a place of his own)
- The killer was white (the victim was white, and this type of crime rarely crossed racial lines)
- The killer would possess pictures or books featuring cruelty to women (the mutilation of the body and the staging of the crime scene were evidence of cruel fantasies)

- The killer was or had been in a mental institution (the mutilation and staging showed
  serious mental illness)
- The killer might be untidy or "weird" in
  some way, and might have made suicide
  attempts in the past (common symptoms
  of serious mental illness)

With the profile in hand, the police reviewed their suspect list and focused on Carmine Calabro, an unemployed man who lived with his father in the Elvesons' building. The police had already interviewed him, but he had an alibi—he had been at a mental hospital receiving treatment at the time of the murder. When police checked the hospital, though, they discovered that security at the institution was poor. Calabro had simply walked out the night before the murder. Calabro turned out to have a history of suicide attempts and a stash of pictures showing women being mistreated. After his arrest, forensic experts examined his teeth. His tooth pattern matched bite marks left on Elveson's body. Calabro was convicted of homicide and sent to prison.

No one can say for certain what role the FBI profile played in the arrest of Carmine Calabro. He had come under suspicion before the profile was developed. Police almost certainly would have checked his alibi eventually, which would have prompted them to take a closer look at him as a suspect. But according to FBI agent John Douglas, who helped develop the profile, the profile itself had spurred detectives to focus their attention on Calabro. Their success in solving this case convinced the New York detectives that profiling was real, and useful.

Years later Laurence Alison, the University of Liverpool researcher, used the Calabro case in his study of how police and forensic professionals interpret profiles. In Alison's experiment, each subject received the case details, the FBI profile, and a description of either Calabro or a fake offender whose characteristics were very different. The subjects rated the profile as about equally accurate whether they applied it to Calabro or the fake offender. At the same time, however, nearly all the police officers and more than half the forensic professionals said that the profile would be useful in the investigation, mainly because it would help narrow the list of suspects.

In the mid-1980s the FBI reviewed 192 cases that had produced criminal profiles. Eighty-eight of those cases had been solved. Profiles had helped investigators identify the subject in fifteen of those cases, or 17 percent of the total. Research is under way to study the role of profiles in solving more recent cases.

People who work in law enforcement and forensic psychology have a range of opinions about the

▲ Do profiles play a major role in putting society's offenders behind bars? The answer may come from research in criminology and psychology.

▲ Investigators gather evidence after a 2002 shooting near Washington, D.C. The victim was the tenth person killed by a sniper who terrorized the region.

value of profiling. A study published in 1990 looked at what police and other investigators thought about FBI profiles they had used. More than 77 percent of the reports were rated as useful. They provided an outside point of view on the case and helped focus the search for the offender. On the other hand, a British survey in 1994 found that 70 percent of police psychologists did not like profiling and doubted its accuracy and usefulness.

Profiling as a formal investigative tool is fairly new. Research into how it works is just beginning. Perhaps such research will make profiling more scientific. Yet some people who work in the field doubt that profiling can ever be purely scientific. Pat Brown, who has worked as a profiler for attorneys, for the media, and in her own investigative agency, views profiling as both an art and a science. A profiler makes guesses based on his or her own mix of experience, common sense, and the facts of the case.

Criminal profiling has won support, and it has also drawn criticism. One thing is clear, however. Profiling has established itself as a tool of modern crime investigation. Since the 1970s criminal profiles have been used in thousands of cases, from serial killings to Internet harassment. With each profile, investigators and criminologists learn more about crime, criminals, and profiling itself.

Computers are involved in a range of crimes, from espionage to harassment. But even anonymous cyber-villains may leave clues for profilers.

CHAPTER THREE

KILLERS, CYBERCRIMINALS, AND MORE

▼ **FROM CAPTURING A "VAMPIRE" TO**
tracking down cybervillains, criminal profiles have helped solve a wide variety of crimes. Dramatic cases of multiple murder tend to receive the most attention, but profiling has been used against other kinds of offenders, too.

▶ BLOOD IN FRESNO

Back in 1978, in the early years of FBI profiling, two profilers helped police catch a killer known as the Vampire of Sacramento. A woman was murdered in her home in the California city. The autopsy of her body showed that the killer had removed her organs and drained some of her blood. He had made no effort to conceal footprints or other traces of his presence.

Profilers Robert Ressler and Russ Vorpagel surveyed the facts and profiled the unsub as white, male, skinny, and in his mid-twenties. They noted that he may have walked around with blood on his clothes and that his residence surely would contain evidence of the crime. The profilers believed that the killer was mentally disturbed, probably to the point of being unable to hold a job or maintain a car. This suggested that the killer probably lived not far from the victim, and that he had received treatment for mental illness.

Then the killer struck a second home, killing three people. He drove off in the victims' car, which police found abandoned. Like the first murder, the trio of killings suggested a deeply disturbed, disorganized mind. The profilers felt that the unsub could not have traveled far from the place where he abandoned the car, and indeed, police found the killer, twenty-seven-year-old Richard Trenton Chase, less than a block away. They discovered body parts and a bloodstained blender in his home. Chase suffered from delusions. His blood was turning to sand, he said, and he needed fresh blood from victims to stay alive.

In the Chase case, profiling proved both accurate and useful. With a large-scale manhunt under way, the police would have visited Chase's home at some point, but investigators were certain that the profile cut down on the time it took them to arrive there.

▶ FROM SNIPERS TO A BURGLAR

In the fall of 2002 a series of highway shootings around Washington, D.C., left ten people dead and three others seriously injured. Authorities hoped that a tool called geographical profiling would help them locate the Beltway Sniper, as the unsub was called.

The idea behind geographic profiling is that the locations of crimes are often related to a location that is important in the criminal's life—a home, workplace,

▲ A methodical crime scene search may produce hard evidence such as a discarded cigarette or shell casing. A profiler, however, also considers the location and geography of the scene.

hideout, or other familiar spot. A geographic profiler assumes that a criminal is likely to choose the easiest site for a crime, and to take the easiest route to it. The criminal is most likely to commit crimes relatively close to home—but not too close. Geographic profiling starts by mapping the crime locations. The next step is to look for areas from which all the mapped locations can easily be reached. Those areas become the starting points for police investigations.

In the Beltway Sniper case, authorities tried a geographic profiling software program called Rigel, developed by a Canadian detective named Kim

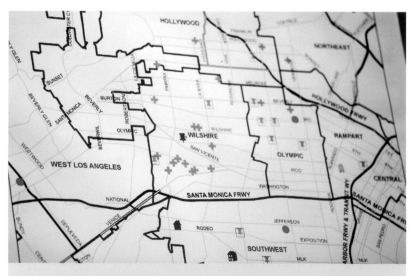

▲ The map shows crime scenes linked to a Los Angeles serial rapist and murderer. Offenders often commit multiple crimes in an area they know well or pass through frequently.

Rossmo. In the end, however, police solved the case through an anonymous tip, having received no useful predictions from the program.

It is possible that the area involved in the Beltway case was too large, and the number of changing circumstances was too great, for Rigel to work properly. Three years later, the same program brought a long-standing burglary case in Irvine, California, to a successful conclusion. For five years police had been looking for a burglar who had robbed more than two hundred homes, stealing jewelry, money, and coin collections. Police called the unsub the Chair Burglar because part of the MO was to put a chair next to any fence near the target house. If the burglar had to make a sudden getaway, the chair would provide a quick boost over the fence.

Authorities finally nabbed the Chair Burglar—who had burglary tools in his home, along with thousands of pieces of loot from the crimes—because the Rigel program had analyzed information about the crimes. This analysis not only predicted where the burglar might live but also pinpointed likely sites of future burglaries. Police started watching the places predicted by the software. Soon they spotted a suspect, who was later arrested and charged with the crimes.

▶ PROFILING COMPUTER CRIMINALS

According to Eoghan Casey, an expert in preventing and solving computer crimes, "Criminal profiling can be most useful when little is known about the offender(s)." This is often the case with crimes carried out over the Internet. The easy anonymity of cyberspace lets offenders use aliases, false addresses, and complicated cover-ups to hide their identities. Even anonymous criminals, however, leave hints that a profiler may be able to use. Casey describes several such cases in *Criminal Profiling*.

When a woman began receiving anonymous death threats by e-mail, investigators could not track the source of the messages. The sender was using an anonymous e-mail service to hide his or her identity. Based on the contents of the messages, however, profilers thought that the offender might work in the same organization as the victim. They also thought that the offender would have tested the anonymous service before sending the threats, just to make sure that the e-mails could not be traced. The best way to do this would be to send himself or herself a message by way of the service.

Investigators searched the Internet traffic records of the entire organization. One other employee, they discovered, had received a single message from the same

▲ Law enforcement officers learn how to collect digital evidence that can be used in court at an FBI training center for computer forensics in California's Silicon Valley.

e-mail service. When they searched that employee's computer they found evidence that linked him to the threats.

Online activity may give a profiler insights into an offender's state of mind. In one case involving a sexual predator who met children online and then lured them into meetings, the profiler reviewed records of the offender's online chats with his victims. The profiler determined that the predator genuinely did not believe he was a threat to children. Instead, he hoped to win their affection. The profiler suggested that the investigators would increase their chances of getting useful information from their suspect by allowing him to think that they were sympathetic to his point of view.

Computers can also help profilers with victimology. Information about the activities and lifestyle of a crime victim is often essential when the victim has died. In the case of Sharon Lopatka, a woman who was killed by a man she met through the Internet, investigators discovered that her online life showed an otherwise hidden interest in dangerous sexual activities. Although in real life Lopatka appeared to be at low risk of becoming a victim of violent crime, her online behavior put her at higher risk. E-mails found in her computer were vital clues, linking her to the man eventually charged with her murder.

▶ THE ROLE OF CRIMINAL PROFILING

Criminal profiling is not a surefire way of identifying an unknown offender. Moreover, the profession does not yet have a clear-cut definition or standards. As a practice it is highly flexible, taking many different forms depending upon the profiler. Profiling often fails to help solve cases, and its accuracy is questionable even when it is credited with a breakthrough.

At the same time, many people in the profiling field hope to establish professional standards.

Criminologists are carrying out research on how pro-files are made and how they are interpreted. This research may help improve profiling's overall accuracy, making profiles more and more helpful.

Most law enforcers and criminologists agree that profiling is far from perfect. But they also feel that profiling has a place in the toolkit of modern crime investigation. Many people—victims and their families as well as police and profilers—might say that any-thing that gets positive results even part of the time is worth trying. In the words of profiler Pat Brown, "[T]he smart investigator will use all the help he can get when the case goes cold. Justice, public safety, and successful case management depend on using all the tools available to us in society today."

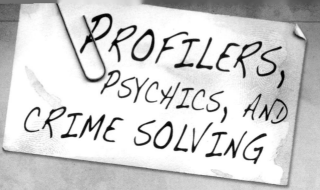

PROFILERS, PSYCHICS, AND CRIME SOLVING

PROFILERS "DON'T GET VIBES or experience psychic flashes while walking around fresh crime scenes," according to the FBI. Instead, the crime analyst's tools are clear, logical thinking, crime-solving experience, and knowledge of facts and statistics about criminal behavior. But what about people who *do* claim to get vibes or flashes? What about psychics who offer information about unsolved crimes or missing people?

A psychic claims to know things that are not available to the ordinary senses. (The psychic's mysterious mental power is sometimes called ESP, for extrasensory perception.) Psychics often say they receive this information from a distance, or by holding an object belonging to a missing person or walking around a crime scene.

Despite much testing, ESP has never been proven to exist. Most scientists think that psychics are, at best, shrewd readers of character with a good understanding of psychology and a lot of common sense. Many psychics sincerely believe in their powers. At worst, however, some psychics have been shown to be frauds or con artists.

Psychics often claim to have solved crimes or provided valuable leads to police or victims' families. In many cases, though, research reveals that the psychic could easily have used methods similar to police methods, such as studying maps, reading witness testimony, or

PSYCHIC ANNETTE MARTIN ATTEMPTS TO RECEIVE INFORMATION FROM A PHOTOGRAPH. THE EXISTENCE OF PSYCHIC POWERS IS UNPROVEN, AND SO IS THEIR ROLE IN CRIME SOLVING.

simply making logical guesses. Some psychics have also been caught misrepresenting themselves, usually by pretending that they helped with highly publicized cases, such as the 1994—1995 murder trial of former football star O.J. Simpson. A California psychic named Carla Baron claimed that she worked with the family of Simpson's slain former wife, but the victim's sister said that no one in the family had ever heard of Baron.

·····

In many cases, psychics are simply wrong. Well-known psychic Sylvia Browne predicted that a missing boy named Shawn Hornbeck would be found dead in a wooded area 20 miles from his home. Instead he was found alive in a house in his hometown. In the case of Elizabeth Smart, a fourteen-year-old Utah girl kidnapped from her home in 2002, police received many psychic tips, none of which were of any value.

Both the FBI and the National Center for Missing and Exploited Children have stated that they do not know of any case that a psychic has helped solve. Critics point out that many famous cases—such as the disappearance of a three-year-old British child named Madeleine McCann during a family vacation in 2007—remain unsolved despite blizzards of useless psychic tips. They also argue that when the media or members of a victim's family pressure law enforcement to follow psychic leads, valuable police time and resources may be drained away from proven, traditional forms of investigation.

Yet some profilers and law enforcement officers claim that psychics can be helpful at times. Former FBI profiler Robert Ressler had said that he consulted psychic Noreen Renier on several cases. He did so informally because, as he says, "the FBI never condoned working with a psychic." In Ressler's view, worthwhile psychic insights come from keen observation and logical thinking, just like the insights of a good detective or profiler.

During the 1980s a police chief in Homestead, Pennsylvania, asked a psychic for help catching a serial rapist. In the end, the offender was captured through regular police work. According to the chief, however, the psychic had genuine, unexplainable knowledge about the case, such as the names of victims who had not yet come forward. He consulted the psychic frequently after that.

Frank Jendesky, a Pennsylvania state trooper, is typical of many in law enforcement in taking a neutral position on the question of psychic powers. He knows of no psychic information that has helped an investigation but says, "We'll sit down and talk with [psychics] when they feel they can help the case. We don't want to be misled. But we have to see what they say." In this view, no lead should be overlooked.

▼ GLOSSARY

autopsy a medical examination of a body for the purpose of determining the cause of death; a forensic autopsy also tries to establish the time and manner of death

criminalistics the study of physical evidence from a crime scene

criminology the study of crime, criminals, and criminal behavior

forensic science the use of scientific knowledge or methods to investigate crimes, identify suspects, and try criminal cases in court

forensics in general, debate or review of any question of fact relating to the law; often used to refer to forensic science

homicide murder

jurisdiction an area or district covered by a particular law enforcement or justice agency; also, can refer to the authorities who investigate different types of crimes (for example, kidnapping is a federal crime, while murder is under state jurisdiction)

medical examiner a public official responsible for determining cause of death; the position requires medical training

modus operandi a Latin phrase meaning "method of operating," used to refer to a criminal's particular procedure or way of committing a crime; often shortened to MO

profiling the process of describing the traits or features of a criminal based on the facts of the crime and the crime scene

prosecutor an attorney who argues the case against an accused criminal, acting on behalf of the people of a state or the federal government

psychiatry the medical treatment of mental, emotional, and behavioral disorders

psychology the study of the mind and of behavior

toxicology the branch of medical and forensic science that deals with drugs, poisons, and harmful substances

trace evidence very small amounts of material, such as carpet fiber, hair, or paint chips, left at the crime scene or detected on the criminal's clothing or body

unsub an unidentified criminal or offender; short for "unknown subject"

victimology the study of crime victims, both as individuals in particular cases and in groups; the victim's traits may point to traits of the offender

▼ FIND OUT MORE

FURTHER READING

Davis, Barbara J. *Criminal Profiling*. Milwaukee, WI : World Almanac Library, 2007.

Esherick, Joan. *Criminal Psychology and Personality Profiling*. Broomall, PA: Mason Crest, 2005.

Funkhluser, John. *Forensic Science for High School Students*. Dubuque, IA: Kendall Hunt, 2005.

Levy, Janet. *Careers in Criminal Profiling*. New York: Rosen Central, 2008.

Mattern, Joanne. *Forensics*. San Diego, CA: Blackbirch Press, 2004.

Platt, Richard. *Crime Scene: The Ultimate Guide to Forensic Science*. New York: Dorling Kindersley, 2003.

Shone, Rob, and Nick Spender. *Solving Crimes through Criminal Profiling*. New York: Rosen Publishing, 2008.

WEBSITES

www.aafs.org/yfsf/index.htm

The website of the American Academy of Forensic Sciences features the Young Forensic Scientists Forum, with information on careers in forensics. The site also links to other Internet resources.

www.fbi.gov/hq/td/academy/bsu/bsu.htm
www.fbi.gov/hq/isd/cirg/ncavc.htm
These FBI websites explain the purpose and func-
tions of the Behavioral Science Unit and the
National Center for the Analysis of Violent
Crime, divisions in which profilers are trained
and employed.

www.johndouglasmindhunter.com
Retired FBI profiler and author John Douglas
maintains this site, with links to many articles by
Douglas and others on subjects such as profiling,
solving cases, and serial killers.

www.sciencenewsforkids.org/articles/20041215/
Feature1.asp
Science News for Kids features this article on
crime labs and what they do, with links to addi-
tional sites and a brief history of forensic science.

www.crimezzz.net/forensic_history/index.htm
The Crimeline page offers a brief timeline of
developments in forensic science from prehistory
to the present.

www.forensicmag.com/

Forensic Magazine's web page features case studies and news about developments in criminalistics and other branches of forensic science.

www.patbrownprofiling.com/

Criminal profiler Pat Brown has worked with law enforcement agencies, attorneys, and businesses. Her website offers articles on such topics as "The 10 Biggest Myths about Serial Killers" and "How to Profile a Terrorist."

▼ BIBLIOGRAPHY

The author found these books and articles especially helpful when researching this volume.

Alison, Laurence, editor. *The Forensic Psychologist's Casebook: Psychological Profiling and Criminal Investigation.* Uffculme, Devon, UK: Willan Publishing, 2005.
——————-, Adrian West, and Alasdair Goodwill. "The Academic and the Practitioner: Pragmatists' View of Offender Profiling." *Psychology, Public Policy, and Law.* 2004, Vol. 10, No. 1–2, pp. 71–101.
——————-, Matthew Smith, and Keith Morgan. "Interpreting the Accuracy of Offender Profiles."*Psychology, Crime, & Law.* 2003, Vol. 9(2), pp. 185–195.
Denevi, Don, editor. *Profiling: Leading Investigators Take You inside the Criminal Mind.* Amherst, NY: Prometheus Books, 2004.
Douglas, John. *Mindhunter: Inside the FBI's Elite Serial Crime Unit.* New York: Scribner, 1995.
Gladwell, Malcolm. "Dangerous Minds: Criminal Profiling Made Easy." *The New Yorker,* November 12, 2007, online at www.newyorker.com/reporting/ 2007/11/12/071112fa_fact_gladwell?

Godwin, Grover Maurice. *Criminal Psychology and Forensic Technology: A Collaborative Approach to Effective Profiling.* Boca Raton, FL: CRC Press, 2000.

Greenwood, Jill K. and Chris Togneri, "Uneasy affiliation: Police and psychics." *Pittsburgh Tribune-Review,* April 13, 2008, online at www.pittsburghlive.com/x/pittsburghtrib/focus/ s_561288.html

James, Stuart H., and Jon J. Nordby, editors. *Forensic Science: An Introduction to Scientific and Investigative Techniques.* 2nd edition. London: CRC Press, 2005.

Kocsis, Richard N. *Criminal Profiling: Principles and Practice.* Totowa, NJ: Humana Press, 2006.

McCrary, Gregg. *The Unknown Darkness: Profiling the Predators among Us.* New York: HarperTorch, 2004.

Nickell, Joe. "The Case of the 'Psychic Detectives.'" *Skeptical Inquirer,* July 2005. Online at www.csicop.org/si/2005-07/i-files.html

Petherick, Wayne. *The Science of Criminal Profiling.* New York: B & N Publishers, 2005.

Science Daily. "Forensic Psychiatrists Discuss
  Limitations Regarding FBI Profiles of Serial
  Killers." Oct. 29, 2006, online at
  www.sciencedaily.com/releases/2006/10/
  061027183522.htm

Turvey, Brent E. *Criminal Profiling: An Introduction to
  Behavioral Evidence Analysis.* Third edition.
  London and New York: Academic Press, 2008.

Winerman, Lea. "Criminal Profiling: The Reality
  behind the Myth." American Psychological
  Association: *Monitor on Psychology,* Vol. 35, No. 7,
  July/August 2004, online at www.apa.org/monitor/
  julaug04/criminal.html

▼ INDEX

▼ ABOUT THE AUTHOR

REBECCA STEFOFF is the author of many books on scientific subjects for young readers. In addition to writing previous volumes in the Forensic Science Investigated series, she has explored the world of evolutionary biology in Marshall Cavendish's Family Trees series; she also wrote *Robot* and *Camera* for Marshall Cavendish's Great Inventions series. After publishing *Charles Darwin and the Evolution Revolution* (Oxford University Press, 1996), she appeared in the *A&E Biography* program on Darwin and his work. Stefoff lives in Portland, Oregon. You can learn more about her books for young readers at **www.rebeccastefoff.com**.